Everyday Comfort Food

*An Easy-To-Follow Guide With Soups,
Snacks, Sides, Appetizers, Lunch, Desserts,
Healthy Farmhouse Dinners*

Melany Holt

Table of Contents

Introduction

If you're picking up this book, you may have been missing out on comfort foods for some time now. I'm happy to say that those times are about to come to an end. You no longer need to give up fluffy dinner rolls, macaroni, and cheese, or your mother's hearty casserole. I'll show you how to put them back on the dinner table.

We all love and care about our favorite comfort foods. They are the foods that replace a warm hug from grandmother. They are our go-to foods on cold winter days, after breakups, and after a bad day. They remind us of our childhood days; they remind us of meals shared with our best friends, crushes, and soul mates.

Packed with vibrant flavors and regional inspirations, this book provides you with an exclusive collection of over 600 international comfort foods. Indulge yourself in the wealth of international comfort foods to explore your new favorites.

It's time to comfort yourself with a hot soothing bowl of your favorite dish and indulge in its delightful flavors. Get ready to curl up in the company of these delicious comfort foods.

The Nostalgia of Comfort Foods

The concept of comforting home cooking is growing rapidly among food enthusiasts. Comfort foods can be prepared in any season. Just one bowl of these around-the-globe comfort foods can bring a smile to your face when you need it most. Ever wondered why our favorite comfort foods taste so great? It has a psychological connection to it. When you prepare your favorite comfort food, it emits its unique aroma. That aroma enters your nasal cavity and reaches your limbic system, which is associated with long-term memory and emotions. When this system senses a familiar aroma, it recognizes its earlier interactions, which triggers pleasure. That is why we crave and love our favorite comfort foods. You do not need an excuse to make them; they are simple and yet never fail to give their warm love. Their soothing aroma is enough to bring everyone together at the dining table.

Comfort food is amazing. What else can evoke childhood memories of family, soothe that homesick feeling, and stitch together a broken heart?

Rainy days are suddenly sunny when you are homebound with the aroma of your mother's pot pie. Sore throats are soothed slurping down a steaming bowl of chicken noodle soup. A stressful day at work fades after you devour a slice of chocolate cake.

Why? Because our senses bring back memories—smells, tastes, textures—that comfort foods radiate straight to our hearts. We are instantly transported. How do you feel thinking about gooey cheese stretching from slices of lasagna, warm spaghetti noodles twirling on grandma's antique fork or that first bite of fluffy pancakes on Sunday morning?

Chapter 1: Breakfast Recipes

1. Italian Chicken Breast

Preparation Time: 10 minutes | Cooking Time: 15 minutes | Servings: 1

Ingredients:

1 chicken breast, skinless and boneless

1 tbsp Italian seasoning

1 tbsp olive oil

1 tsp garlic, minced

Pepper

Salt

Directions:

Coat chicken with oil and rub with Italian seasoning, garlic, pepper, and salt.

Place the dehydrating tray in a multi-level air fryer basket and place basket in the instant pot.

Place chicken on the dehydrating tray.

Seal pot with air fryer lid and select air fry mode then set the temperature to 350ºF and timer for 15 minutes.

Turn chicken halfway through.

Serve and enjoy.

Nutrition:

Calories 295, Fat 21g, Carbohydrates 2.5g, Sugar 1.3g,

Protein 24g, Cholesterol 82mg.

2. Zucchini Patties

Preparation Time: 10 minutes | Cooking Time: 30 minutes | Servings: 6

Ingredients:

1 egg, lightly beaten

1/2 cup breadcrumbs

2 tbsp onion, minced

1 cup zucchini, shredded

1/4 cup parmesan cheese, grated

1/2 tbsp mayonnaise

Pepper

Salt

Directions:

Add all ingredients into the bowl and mix until well combined.

Place the dehydrating tray in a multi-level air fryer basket and place basket in the instant pot.

Make small patties from the zucchini mixture and place them on a dehydrating tray.

Seal pot with air fryer lid and select bake mode then set the temperature to 380°F and timer for 25 minutes.

Turn patties halfway through. Serve and enjoy.

Nutrition:

Calories 67, Fat 2.5g, Carbohydrates 7.9g, Sugar 1.2g, Protein 3.6g, Cholesterol 30mg.

3. Spinach and Eggs

Preparation time: 25 minutes | Cooking Time: 30 minutes | Servings: 4

Ingredients:

3 cups baby spinach

12 eggs; whisked

1 tbsp. Olive oil

½ tsp. Smoked paprika

Salt and black pepper to taste.

Directions:

Take a bowl and mix all the ingredients except the oil and whisk them well.

Heat your air fryer at 360°F, add the oil, heat it, add the

eggs and spinach mix, cover, cook for 20 minutes.

Divide between plates and serve

Nutrition:

Calories 220, Fat 11g, Fiber 3g, Carbs 4g, Protein 6g.

4. Bell pepper eggs

Preparation time: 25 minutes | Cooking Time: 30 minutes | Servings: 4

Ingredients:

4 medium green bell peppers

¼ medium onion; peeled and chopped

3 oz. Cooked ham; chopped

8 large eggs.

1 cup mild cheddar cheese

Directions:

Cut the tops off each bell pepper. Remove the seeds and the white membranes with a small knife.

Place ham and onion into each pepper

Crack 2 eggs into each pepper. Top with ¼ cup cheese per pepper.

Place into the air fryer basket

Adjust the temperature to 390°F and set the timer for 15 minutes.

When fully cooked, peppers will be tender and eggs will be firm. Serve immediately.

Nutrition:

Calories 314, Protein 24.9g, Fiber 1.7g, Fat 18.6g, Carbs 6.3g.

5. Cajun Cheese Zucchini

Preparation Time: 10 minutes | Cooking Time: 1 minute

| Servings: 4

Ingredients:

4 zucchinis, sliced

1/4 cup parmesan cheese, grated

1/2 cup water

1 tbsp butter

1 tsp garlic powder

1/2 tsp paprika 2 tbsp Cajun seasoning

Directions:

Add all ingredients except cheese into the inner pot of

instant pot duo crisp and stir well.

Seal the pot with a pressure-cooking lid and cook on high for 1 minute.

Once done, release pressure using a quick release. Remove lid.

Top with parmesan cheese and serve.

Nutrition:

Calories 80, Fat 4.6g, Carbohydrates 7.4g, Sugar 3.6g, Protein 4.6g, Cholesterol 12mg.

6. **Spinach Feta Muffins**

Preparation Time: 10 minutes | Cooking Time: 20 minutes | Servings: 6

Ingredients:

3 eggs

1/2 tsp olive oil

1/2 tsp dried oregano

1/2 tsp dried basil

1 tbsp olives, diced

1/4 cup sun-dried tomatoes, diced

2 tbsp spinach, cooked

1/4 cup egg whites

1 tbsp feta cheese, crumbled

Pepper

Salt

Directions:

In a bowl, whisk eggs, oil, and egg whites until well combined.

Add remaining ingredients and stir well.

Pour egg mixture into the silicone muffin molds and place it in the air fryer basket. place basket in the pot.

Seal the pot with an air fryer lid and select bake mode and cook at 350ºF for 20 minutes.Serve and enjoy.

Nutrition:

Calories 55, Fat 3g, Carbohydrates 1.6g, Sugar 0.3g, Protein 4g, Cholesterol 83mg.

7. Pesto Cheese Chicken

Preparation Time: 10 minutes | Cooking Time: 35 minutes | Servings: 4

Ingredients:

4 chicken breasts, skinless, boneless, and cut in half

1 cup mozzarella cheese, shredded

2 large tomatoes, sliced

1/2 cup basil pesto

Pepper

Salt

Directions:

Line instant pot air fryer basket with aluminum foil and

spray with cooking spray.

In a bowl, mix pesto and chicken until coated.

Place chicken in air fryer basket and place basket in the pot.

Seal the pot with an air fryer lid and select bake mode and cook at 400ºF for 35 minutes.

Remove chicken from pot and top with cheese and tomatoes.

Serve and enjoy.

Nutrition:

Calories 314, Fat 11g, Carbohydrates 4g, Sugar 2g, Protein 45g, Cholesterol 134mg.

8. Meatballs

Preparation Time: 10 minutes | Cooking Time: 25 minutes | Servings: 6

Ingredients:

2 lbs ground beef 2 tbsp parsley, chopped

2 tbsp green onion, chopped

1/4 cup bell pepper, roasted and chopped

1/4 cup olives, chopped

1/4 tsp onion powder

1/2 tsp garlic powder

1/4 cup feta cheese, crumbled

1/4 cup sun-dried tomatoes, chopped

1/2 tsp black pepper

1/2 tsp salt

Directions:

Line instant pot air fryer basket with parchment paper or foil.

Add all ingredients into the mixing bowl and mix until combined.

Make small meatballs from the mixture and place them into the air fryer basket. Place basket in the pot.

Seal the pot with an air fryer lid and select bake mode and cook at 400ºF for 25 minutes.Serve and enjoy.

Nutrition:

Calories 315, Fat 11g, Carbohydrates 3g, Sugar 0.7g, Protein 46g, Cholesterol 140mg.

Chapter 2: Lunch Recipes

9. Beef Cheesy Potatoes

Preparation Time: 5 minutes | Cooking Time: 20 minutes Serving: 4

Ingredients:

1 ½ pounds ground beef

6 large potatoes, peeled and chopped 2 cups cheddar cheese, shredded ¾ cup chicken broth 1 tablespoon Italian seasoning mix Salt and pepper to taste

Directions:

Press the Sauté button on the Instant Pot and stir in the beef. Brown the meat until some of the oil has rendered.

Add the rest of the ingredients.

Close Instant Pot, press the Manual button, choose high settings, and set the time to 20 minutes.

Once done cooking, do a QPR. Serve and enjoy.

Nutrition:

Calories 806, Carbohydrates 66.8g, Protein 53.4g, Fat 35.6g, Sugar 3.5g, Sodium 609mg.

10. Sweet Potato Chili Recipe

Preparation Time: 5 minutes | Cooking Time: 30 minutes

Serving: 4

Ingredients:

1 teaspoon olive oil

1 onion, diced

3 cloves of garlic, minced

½ pound ground pork

1-pound ground beef

1 large sweet potato, peeled and cut into ½" pieces

3 celery stalks, sliced

3 ½ cups crushed tomatoes

1 tablespoon Worcestershire sauce

1 teaspoon cumin

1 teaspoon chili powder

Salt and pepper to taste

Directions:

Press the Sauté button on the Instant Pot and heat the olive oil. Sauté the onion and garlic until fragrant.

Stir in the pork and beef and allow to brown for 5 minutes.

Add the rest of the ingredients.

Close Instant Pot, press the Manual button, choose high settings, and set the time to 20 minutes.

Once done cooking, do a QPR.

Serve and enjoy.

Nutrition:

Calories 447, Carbohydrates 16.4g, Protein 36.9g, Fat
25.9g, Sugar 4.1g, Sodium 172mg.

11. Instant Pot Stuffed Peppers

Preparation Time: 5 minutes | Cooking Time: 40 minutes

Serving: 4

Ingredients:

½ pound ground beef

1/3 cup diced onions

1 ½ cup spaghetti sauce

½ teaspoon garlic salt

2 cups cooked rice

8 bell peppers, cut the top, and remove the seeds

1 cup mozzarella cheese, shredded

Directions:

Press the Sauté button on the Instant Pot and add the beef and onions. Stir constantly.

Stir in the spaghetti sauce and season with garlic salt.

Close Instant Pot, press the Manual cook button, choose high settings, and set time to 10 minutes.

Once done cooking, do a QPR.

Transfer into a bowl and add the cooked rice. Stir to combine. Pack the mixture into hollow bell peppers and top with mozzarella cheese.

Place a trivet in the Instant Pot and pour water. Place the stuffed bell peppers on the trivet and close the lid. Press the Steam button and cook for 10 minutes.

Serve and enjoy.

Nutrition:

Calories 265, Carbohydrates 32g, Protein 12g, Fat 9g,

Sugar 10g, Sodium 930mg.

12. **Braised Brisket**

Preparation Time: 5 minutes | Cooking Time: 30 minutes

Serving: 4

Ingredients:

2 pounds beef brisket, cut into 4 pieces

Salt and pepper to taste

2 cups sliced onion

½ cup of water

2 tablespoons tomato paste

2 tablespoons Worcestershire sauce

2 teaspoons liquid smoke

Directions:

Put all ingredients in the Instant Pot. Mix all ingredients to combine everything.

Close Instant Pot, press pressure cook button, choose high settings and set time to 60 minutes.

Once done cooking, do a QPR.

Serve and enjoy.

Nutrition:

Calories 490, Carbohydrates 9.9g, Protein 34.5g, Fat 33.9g, Sugar 4.8g, Sodium 885mg.

13. Instant Pot Corned Beef and Cabbages

Preparation Time: 5 minutes | Cooking Time: 30 minutes

Serving: 4

Ingredients:

6 cloves of garlic, chopped 1 onion, quartered

2 ½ pounds corned beef brisket, cut in large slices

12-oz. beer 2 cups of water 3 carrots, roughly chopped

2 potatoes, chopped 1 head cabbage, cut into four pieces

Directions:

In the Instant Pot, place the garlic, onion, corned beef

brisket, beer, and water. Season with salt and pepper to taste.

Close Instant Pot, press the Manual button, choose high settings, and set time to 50 minutes.

Once done cooking, do a QPR.

Open the lid and take out the meat. Shred the meat using a fork and place it back into the Instant Pot.

Stir in the vegetables. Close the lid and seal the vent and press the Manual button. Cook for another 10 minutes.

Do QPR. Serve and enjoy.

Nutrition:

Calories 758, Carbohydrates 45.8g, Protein 43.1g, Fat 44.7g, Sugar 8.7g, Sodium 940mg.

14. Beer Mustard Ham

Preparation Time: 5 minutes | Cooking Time: 60 minutes

Serving: 10-12

Ingredients:

½ teaspoon ground black pepper

3-pound bone-in ham chunk

2 bottles of beer

¾ cup Dijon mustard

4 sprigs of rosemary

Directions:

Take your Instant Pot and place it over a dry kitchen

platform.

Open the lid and add the ham. Pour the beer and add the mustard, pepper, and rosemary.

Lock the top lid and make sure that the valve is sealed properly.

Select "Meat/Stew" cooking function. Set the cooking time to 60 minutes.

Your Instant Pot will start building the pressure and begin the cooking cycle after a sufficient level of pressure is reached.

After the cooking time is over, press the "Cancel" setting, and then press "NPR" for the natural release of the internal pressure. It takes around 10 minutes to release the pressure naturally.

Open the top lid, slice the meat, and add back to the pot, let it infuse the flavors for a few minutes.

Transfer the meat to your serving plates and drizzle the remaining sauce on top.

Serve and enjoy the recipe.

Nutrition:

Calories 143, Total Carbohydrates 12g, Fiber 0.5g, Saturated Fat 23g, Trans Fat 0g, Protein 6g, Sodium 231g.

15. Green Bean Mushroom Pork

Preparation Time: 5 minutes | Cooking Time: 30 minutes

Serving: 4

Ingredients:

½ cup onions, diced

3 tablespoons garlic, minced

8 ounces white button mushrooms, sliced

4 cups green beans, halved

1 tablespoon olive oil

4 pork chops

2 cups chicken broth

¼ cup honey

½ cup Dijon mustard

Pepper and salt as per your taste preference

1 tablespoon cornstarch + 2 tablespoons water

Directions:

Take your Instant Pot and place it over a dry kitchen platform.

Open the lid and select the "Sauté" cooking function.

Add the oil and chops into the pot; cook to soften and sear evenly.

Add the onion and garlic; sauté for a few minutes.

Add the remaining ingredients except for the cornstarch mix; gently stir.

Lock the top lid and make sure that the valve is sealed

properly.

Select "Meat/Stew" cooking function. Set the cooking time to 30 minutes.

Your Instant Pot will start building the pressure and begin the cooking cycle after a sufficient level of pressure is reached.

After the cooking time is over, press the "Cancel" setting, and then press "NPR" for the natural release of the internal pressure. It takes around 10 minutes to release the pressure naturally.

Open the top lid, mix in the cornstarch mix, and stir thoroughly.

Transfer the meal to your serving bowls.

Serve and enjoy the recipe.

Nutrition:

Calories 364, Total Carbohydrates 10g, Fiber 3g, Saturated Fat 18g, Trans Fat 0g, Protein 27g, Sodium 534g.

16. Corned Beef

Preparation time: 10 minutes | Cooking Time: 60 minutes | Servings: 6

Ingredients:

4 pounds beef brisket

2 oranges, sliced

2 garlic cloves, peeled and minced

2 yellow onions, peeled and sliced thin

11 ounces celery, sliced thin

1 tablespoon dried dill

3 bay leaves

4 cinnamon sticks, cut into halves

Salt and ground black pepper, to taste

17 ounces of water

Directions:

Put the beef in a bowl, add some water to cover, set aside to soak for a few hours, drain and transfer to the Instant Pot.

Add the celery, orange slices, onions, garlic, bay leaves, dill, cinnamon, dill, salt, pepper, and water. Stir, cover the Instant Pot and cook on the Meat/Stew setting for 50 minutes.

Release the pressure, set the beef aside to cool for 5 minutes, transfer to a cutting board, slice, and divide among plates.

Drizzle the juice and vegetables from the Instant Pot

over beef and serve.

Nutrition:

Calories 251, Fat 3.14g, Fiber 0g, Carbs 1g, Protein 7g.

17. Beef Bourguignon

Preparation time: 15 minutes | Cooking Time: 30 minutes | Servings: 6

Ingredients:

10 pounds round steak, cut into small cubes

2 carrots, peeled and sliced

½ cup beef stock

1 cup dry red wine

3 bacon slices, chopped

8 ounces mushrooms, cut into quarters

2 tablespoons white flour

12 pearl onions

2 garlic cloves, peeled and minced

¼ teaspoon dried basil

Salt and ground black pepper, to taste

Directions:

Set the Instant Pot on Sauté mode, add the bacon, and

brown it for 2 minutes.

Add the beef pieces, stir, and brown for 5 minutes.

Add the flour and stir very well.

Add the salt, pepper, wine, stock, onions, garlic, and

basil, stir, cover, and cook on the Meat/Stew setting for

20 minutes.

Release the pressure, uncover the Instant Pot, add the

mushrooms and carrots, cover the Instant Pot again,

and cook on the Manual setting for 5 minutes.

Release the pressure again, divide the beef bourguignon among plates, and serve.

Nutrition:

Calories 442, Fat 17.2g, Fiber 3g, Carbs 16g, Protein 39g.

18.   Beef Chili

Preparation time: 10 minutes | Cooking Time: 40 minutes | Servings: 6

Ingredients:

1½ pounds ground beef

1 sweet onion, peeled and chopped

Salt and ground black pepper, to taste

16 ounces mixed beans, soaked overnight, and drained

28 ounces canned diced tomatoes

17 ounces beef stock

12 ounces beer

6 garlic cloves, peeled and chopped

7 jalapeño peppers, diced

2 tablespoons vegetable oil

4 carrots, peeled and chopped

3 tablespoons chili powder

1 bay leaf

1 teaspoon chili powder

Directions:

Set the Instant Pot on Sauté mode, add half of the oil, and heat it.

Add the beef, stir, brown for 8 minutes, and transfer to a bowl.

Add the rest of the oil to the Instant Pot and heat it.

Add the carrots, onion, jalapeños, and garlic, stir, and sauté for 4 minutes.

Add the beer and tomatoes and stir.

Add the beans, bay leaf, stock, chili powder, chili powder, salt, pepper, and beef, stir, cover and cook on the Bean/Chili setting for 25 minutes.

Release the pressure naturally, uncover the Instant Pot, stir chili, transfer to bowls, and serve.

Nutrition:

Calories 272, Fat 5g, Fiber 0g, Carbs 32g, Protein 25g.

19. Chili Con Carne

Preparation time: 10 minutes | Cooking Time: 30 minutes | Servings: 4

Ingredients:

1-pound ground beef

1 yellow onion, peeled and chopped

4 tablespoons extra virgin olive oil

Salt and ground black pepper, to taste

2 garlic cloves, peeled and minced

1 bay leaf

4 ounces kidney beans, soaked overnight and drained

1 teaspoon tomato paste

8 ounces canned diced tomatoes

1 tablespoon chili powder

½ teaspoon cumin

5 ounces of water

Directions:

Set the Instant Pot on Sauté mode, add 1 tablespoon oil, and heat it.

Add the meat, brown for a few minutes, and transfer to a bowl.

Add the rest of the oil to the Instant Pot and also heat it.

Add the onion and garlic, stir, and cook for 3 minutes.

Return the beef to the pot, add the bay leaf, beans, tomato paste, tomatoes, chili powder, cumin, salt, pepper, and water, stir, cover, and cook on the

Bean/Chili setting for 18 minutes.

Release the pressure, uncover the Instant Pot, discard bay leaf, divide chili among bowls, and serve.

Nutrition:

Calories 256, Fat 8g, Fiber 1g, Carbs 22g, Protein 25g.

20.   **Beef Curry**

Preparation time: 10 minutes | Cooking Time: 20 minutes | Servings: 4

Ingredients:

2 pounds beef steak, cubed

2 tablespoons extra virgin olive oil

3 potatoes, diced

1 tablespoon Dijon mustard

2½ tablespoons curry powder

2 yellow onions, peeled and chopped

2 garlic cloves, peeled and minced

10 ounces canned coconut milk

2 tablespoons tomato sauce

Salt and ground black pepper, to taste

Directions:

Set the Instant Pot on Sauté mode, add the oil, and heat it.

Add the onions and garlic, stir and cook for 4 minutes.

Add the potatoes and mustard, stir, and cook for 1 minute.

Add the beef, stir, and brown on all sides.

Add the curry powder, salt, and pepper, stir, and cook for 2 minutes.

Add the coconut milk and tomato sauce, stir, cover the Instant Pot, and cook on the Meat/Stew setting for 10 minutes.

Release the pressure, uncover the Instant Pot, divide

curry among plates, and serve.

Nutrition:

Calories 434, Fat 20g, Fiber 2.9g, Carbs 14g, Protein:

27.5g.

21. Beef Stroganoff

Preparation time: 10 minutes | Cooking Time: 25 minutes | Servings: 4

Ingredients:

10 pounds beef, cut into small cubes

1 yellow onion, peeled and chopped

2½ tablespoons vegetable oil

1½ tablespoons white flour

2 garlic cloves, peeled and minced

4 ounces mushrooms, sliced

1½ tablespoon tomato paste

Salt and ground black pepper, to taste

3 tablespoons Worcestershire sauce

13 ounces beef stock

8 ounces sour cream

Egg noodles, already cooked, for serving

Directions:

Put the beef, salt, pepper, and flour in a bowl and toss to coat.

Set the Instant Pot on Sauté mode, add the oil, and heat it.

Add the meat and brown it on all sides.

Add the onion, garlic, mushrooms, Worcestershire sauce, stock, and tomato paste, stir well, cover the Instant Pot and cook on the Meat/Stew setting for 20 minutes.

Release the pressure, uncover the Instant Pot, add the sour cream, more salt, and pepper, stir well, divide among plates on top of egg noodles and serve.

Nutrition:

Calories 335, Fat 18.4g, Fiber 1.3g, Carbs 22.5g, Protein 20.1g.

22. **Moist Cream Cheese Muffins**

Preparation Time: 10 minutes | Cooking Time: 20 minutes | Servings: 5

Ingredients:

1 egg

1/4 cup Erythritol

4 oz cream cheese

1/2 tsp ground cinnamon

1/4 tsp vanilla

Directions:

In a bowl, beat together cream cheese, vanilla, Erythritol, and eggs until fluffy.

Pour batter into the silicone muffin molds.

Place silicone muffin molds into the instant pot air fryer basket and place the basket in the pot.

Seal the pot with an air fryer lid and select bake mode and cook at 350°F for 20 minutes.

Serve and enjoy.

Nutrition:

Calories 93, Fat 8g, Carbohydrates 11g, Sugar 12g, Protein 2g, Cholesterol 55mg.

23.   Parmesan Salmon

Preparation Time: 10 minutes | Cooking Time: 15 minutes | Servings: 4

Ingredients:

4 salmon fillets

1/4 cup parmesan cheese, grated

1/4 cup walnuts 1 tsp olive oil 1 tbsp lemon rind

Pepper Salt

Directions:

Line instant pot air fryer basket with parchment paper or foil.

Place salmon in the air fryer basket and place basket in

the pot.

Add walnuts into the food processor and process until finely ground.

Mix ground walnuts with cheese, oil, and lemon rind. Stir well.

Spread walnut mixture over the salmon fillets and press gently.

Seal the pot with an air fryer lid and select bake mode and cook at 400ºF for 15 minutes.

Serve and enjoy.

Nutrition:

Calories 420, Fat 26g, Carbohydrates 2g, Sugar 0.3g, Protein 45g, Cholesterol 97mg.

24. Bok Choy And Butter Sauce

Preparation time: 20 minutes | Cooking Time: 15 minutes | Servings: 4

Ingredients:

2 bok choy heads; trimmed and cut into strips

1 tbsp. Butter; melted

2 tbsp. Chicken stock

1 tsp. Lemon juice

1 tbsp. Olive oil

A pinch of salt and black pepper

Directions:

In a pan that fits your air fryer, mix all the ingredients,

toss, introduce the pan in the air fryer, and cook at

380°F for 15 minutes.

Divide between plates and serve as a side dish

Nutrition:

Calories 141, Fat 3, Fiber 2g, Carbs 4g, Protein 3g.

25. Goat Cheese Cauliflower

Preparation time: 25 minutes | Cooking Time: 15 minutes | Servings: 4

Ingredients:

8 cups cauliflower florets; roughly chopped.

4 bacon strips; chopped.

10 oz. Goat cheese, crumbled

¼ cup soft cream cheese

½ cup spring onions; chopped.

1 tbsp. Garlic; minced

Salt and black pepper to taste.

Cooking spray

Directions:

Grease a baking pan that fits the air fryer with the cooking spray and mix all the ingredients except the goat cheese into the pan.

Sprinkle the cheese on top, introduce the pan in the machine and cook at 400°F for 20 minutes

Divide between plates and serve as a side dish.

Nutrition:

Calories 203, Fat 13g, Fiber 2g, Carbs 5g, Protein 9g.

26. Dill Red Cabbage

Preparation time: 25 minutes | Cooking Time: 15 minutes | Servings: 4

Ingredients:

30 oz. Red cabbage; shredded

4 oz. Butter; melted

1 tbsp. Red wine vinegar

2 tbsp. Dill; chopped.

1 tsp. Cinnamon powder

A pinch of salt and black pepper

Directions:

In a pan that fits your air fryer, mix the cabbage with the

rest of the ingredients, toss put the pan in the machine,

and cook at 390°F for 20 minutes

Divide between plates and serve as a side dish.

Nutrition:

Calories 201, Fat 17g, Fiber 2g, Carbs 5g, Protein 5g.

27. Radishes and Sesame Seeds

Preparation time: 20 minutes | Cooking Time: 15 minutes | Servings: 4

Ingredients:

20 radishes; halved

2 spring onions; chopped.

3 green onions; chopped.

2 tbsp. Olive oil 1 tbsp. Olive oil

3 tsp. Black sesame seeds

Salt and black pepper to taste.

Directions:

Take a bowl and mix all the ingredients and toss well.

Put the radishes in your air fryer's basket, cook at 400°F for 15 minutes, divide between plates and serve as a side dish

Nutrition:

Calories 150, Fat 4g, Fiber 2g, Carbs 3g, Protein 5g.

Chapter 3: Dinner Recipes

28.   Kale Beef Soup

Preparation Time: 10 minutes | Cooking Time: 13 minutes | Servings: 6

Ingredients:

1 lb ground beef

1/4 tsp chili powder

1/2 cup coconut milk

8 cups beef broth

1 tbsp garlic, minced

1 onion, diced

3 cups kale, chopped

Pepper

Salt

Directions:

Add ground beef, garlic, and onion into the instant pot

duo crisp and set pot on sauté mode.

Cook ground beef until browned.

Add chili powder, broth, pepper, and salt and stir well.

Seal the pot with a pressure-cooking lid and cook on high pressure for 8 minutes.

Once done, release pressure using a quick release. Remove lid.

Add coconut milk and kale and stir until kale is wilted.

Serve and enjoy.

Nutrition:

Calories 264, Fat 11.4g, Carbohydrates 8.1g, Sugar 2.4g, Protein 31.2g, Cholesterol 68mg.

29. Cabbage Beef Soup

Preparation Time: 10 minutes | Cooking Time: 30 minutes | Servings: 8

Ingredients:

28 oz can tomato, diced

1 tsp dried thyme

1 tsp dried oregano

1 tbsp olive oil

1/2 cup carrots, diced

1/2 cup onion, diced

1 cup cauliflower rice

4 cups beef stock

5 cups cabbage, chopped

1 lb ground beef

28 oz can tomato, diced

1 1/2 tsp salt

Directions:

Add oil into the instant pot duo crisp and set pot on sauté mode.

Add meat and cook until browned.

Add carrots and onion and cook for 5 minutes.

Add remaining ingredients and stir well.

Seal the pot with a pressure-cooking lid and cook on high pressure for 20 minutes.

Once done, allow to release pressure naturally.

Remove lid.

Stir well and serve hot.

Nutrition:

Calories 249, Fat 5.9g, Carbohydrates 24.8g, Sugar 15g,

Protein 23.6g, Cholesterol 51mg.

30. Easy Chicken Salsa Soup

Preparation Time: 10 minutes | Cooking Time: 20 minutes | Servings: 6

Ingredients:

1 lb chicken breast, skinless and boneless

4 cups chicken broth

15 oz jar salsa

Pepper

Salt

Directions:

Add all ingredients into the instant pot duo crisp and stir well.

Seal the pot with a pressure-cooking lid and cook on high pressure for 20 minutes.

Once done, allow to release pressure naturally. Remove lid.

Remove chicken from pot and shred using a fork.

Return shredded chicken to the pot and stir well.

Serve and enjoy.

Nutrition:

Calories 135, Fat 2.8g, Carbohydrates 5.4g, Sugar 2.8g, Protein 19.3g, Cholesterol 48mg.

31. Spring Chicken Soup

Preparation Time: 10 minutes | Cooking Time: 8 minutes | Servings: 6

Ingredients:

2 cups cooked chicken, shredded

1/2 lemon juice

2 tbsp basil, chopped

1/2 tsp dried rosemary

2 tsp Italian seasoning

8 cups chicken broth

2 cups leeks, sliced

1 small onion, diced

1 zucchini, diced

1 tsp garlic, minced

1 tbsp olive oil

1/4 tsp pepper

1 1/2 tsp salt

Directions:

Add oil into the instant pot duo crisp and set pot on sauté mode.

Add leeks, onion, zucchini, and garlic and sauté for 3-4 minutes.

Add broth, rosemary, Italian seasoning, chicken, pepper, and salt, and stir well.

Seal the pot with a pressure-cooking lid and cook on high pressure for 4 minutes.

Once done, allow to release pressure naturally for 5 minutes then release remaining pressure using a quick release. Remove lid.

Add fresh herbs and lemon juice and stir well.

Serve and enjoy.

Nutrition:

Calories 177, Fat 6.2g, Carbohydrates 8.2g, Sugar 3.4g, Protein 21.1g, Cholesterol 37mg.

32. Garlicky Pork Roast

Preparation time: 10 minutes | Cooking Time: 35 minutes | Servings: 2

Ingredients:

1 lb pork roast

1 tbsp basil

1 1/2 tbsp soy sauce

2 tbsp grated parmesan cheese

2 tbsp honey

3 garlic cloves, minced

1/2 cup chicken stock

1/2 tbsp cornstarch

1/2 tbsp olive oil

Salt

Directions:

Add all ingredients into the instant pot and stir well.

Seal pot with lid and cook on meat mode for 35 minutes.

Once done then allow to release pressure naturally then

open the lid.

Stir and serve.

Nutrition:

Calories 578, Fat 47.1g, Carbohydrates 0.5g, Sugar 0.4g,

Protein 36.3g, Cholesterol 138mg.

33. Orange Pulled Pork

Preparation time: 10 minutes | Cooking Time: 30 minutes | Servings: 8

Ingredients:

2 lbs pork shoulder roast, cut into chunks

1/4 cup fresh lime juice

1 cup of orange juice,

1 bay leaf

3/4 tsp ground cumin

2 tbsp olive oil 1/4 tsp pepper 1 tsp salt

Directions:

Add oil into the instant pot and set the pot on sauté

mode.

Season meat with pepper and salt and place into the pot and cook until browned.

Add cumin, bay leaf, lime juice, orange juice, and salt and stir well.

Seal pot with lid and cook on manual high pressure for 25 minutes.

Once done then allow to release pressure naturally then open the lid. Discard bay leaf from pot.

Shred the meat using a fork and serve.

Nutrition:

Calories 337, Fat 26.7g, Carbohydrates 3.7g, Sugar 2.6g, Protein 19.4g, Cholesterol 80mg.

34. Pork with Cabbage

Preparation time: 10 minutes | Cooking Time: 10 minutes | Servings: 4

Ingredients:

1 1/4 lbs pork loin, boneless and cut into cubes

1/2 tsp pepper

1/4 tsp fennel seeds

1 tbsp vinegar

1 cup chicken stock

1 tsp dried dill weed

1/2 small cabbage, cored and cut into wedges

1 onion, cut into wedges

2 tsp olive oil

Directions:

Add oil into the instant pot and set the pot on sauté mode.

Add onion and sauté for 2 minutes.

Add meat and cook for 3 minutes.

Add cabbage and stir well.

In a small bowl, mix dill weed, pepper, and fennel seeds and sprinkle over cabbage.

Pour vinegar and stock into the pot.

Seal pot with lid and cook on manual high pressure for 5 minutes.

Once done then allow to release pressure naturally then open the lid.

Serve and enjoy.

Nutrition:

Calories 382, Fat 22.3g, Carbohydrates 3.8g, Sugar 1.7g,

Protein 39.4g, Cholesterol 113mg.

35. Salsa Pork

Preparation time: 10 minutes | Cooking Time: 15 minutes | Servings: 4

Ingredients:

2 lbs pork shoulder, boneless and cut into chunks

3 tbsp fresh cilantro, chopped

1/2 cup chicken stock

1/2 tsp ground cumin 1 1/2 tbsp honey

14.5 oz can tomato, drained and diced

14 oz salsa 1/2 tsp dried oregano Pepper Salt

Directions:

Season meat with pepper and salt.

Add meat, stock, oregano, cumin, honey, tomatoes, and salsa to the pot.

Seal pot with lid and cook on manual high pressure for 15 minutes.

Once done then allow to release pressure naturally then open the lid.

Shred the meat using a fork.

Garnish with cilantro and serve.

Nutrition:

Calories 738, Fat 48.8g, Carbohydrates 18.3g, Sugar 13.1g, Protein 55.5g, Cholesterol 204mg.

36. Pork Fajitas

Preparation time: 10 minutes | Cooking Time: 20 minutes | Servings: 6

Ingredients:

1 3/4 lbs. pork loin sirloin chops, cut into strips

1 onion, sliced

2 bell pepper, cut into strips

1 1/2 tbsp Italian seasoning

1/2 cup chicken stock

2 tbsp fresh lime juice oz salsa

Directions:

Add all ingredients into the instant pot and stir well.

Seal pot with lid and cook on manual high pressure for

1 minute.

Once done then allow to release pressure naturally for

10 minutes then release using the quick-release method.

Open the lid.

Stir and serve.

Nutrition:

Calories 369, Fat 19.7g, Carbohydrates 9.2g, Sugar 5.1g,

Protein 37.8g, Cholesterol 108mg.

37.   Beef & Lemon Schnitzel for One

Preparation time: 5 minutes | Cooking Time: 12 minutes | Servings: 1

Ingredients:

2 tbsp oil

2–3 oz breadcrumbs

1 whisked egg in a saucer/soup plate

1 beef schnitzel

1 freshly picked lemon

Directions:

Preparing the ingredients. Mix the oil and breadcrumbs until loose and crumbly.

Dip the meat into the egg, then into the crumbs.

Make sure that it is evenly covered.

Air frying. Gently place in the instant crisp air fryer basket, close the air fryer lid and cook at 350° f (preheat if needed until done).

The timing will depend on the thickness of the schnitzel, but for a relatively thin one, it should take roughly 12 min.

Serve with a lemon half and a garden salad.

38. Crispy Beef Schnitzel

Preparation time: 5 minutes | Cooking Time: 12 minutes | Servings: 1

Ingredients:

1 beef schnitzel

Salt and ground black pepper, to taste

2 tablespoons olive oil

1/3 cup breadcrumbs

1 egg, whisked

Directions:

Preparing the ingredients. Season the schnitzel with salt and black pepper.

In a mixing bowl, combine the oil and breadcrumbs. In

another shallow bowl, beat the egg until frothy.

Dip the schnitzel in the egg; then, dip it in the oil mixture.

Close air fryer lid.

Air-fry at 350ºF for 12 minutes. Enjoy!

39. Simple Steak

Preparation time: 6minutes | Cooking Time: 14 minutes

| Servings: 2

Ingredients:

½ pound quality cuts steak

Salt and freshly ground black pepper, to taste

Directions:

Preparing the ingredients. Preheat the instant crisp air fryer to 390ºF.Rub the steak with salt and pepper evenly.

Air frying. Place the steak in the instant crisp air fryer basket, close the air fryer lid and cook for about 14 minutes crispy.

40. Garlic-Cumin and Orange Juice Marinated Steak

Preparation time: 6 minutes | Cooking Time: 60 minutes | Servings: 4

Ingredients:

¼ cup of orange juice

1 teaspoon ground cumin

2 pounds skirt steak, trimmed from excess fat

2 tablespoons lime juice

2 tablespoons olive oil

4 cloves of garlic, minced

Salt and pepper to taste

Directions:

Preparing the ingredients. Place all ingredients in a mixing bowl and allow to marinate in the fridge for at least 2 hours

Preheat the instant crisp air fryer to 390°f.

Place the grill pan accessory in the instant crisp air fryer.

Air frying. Close air fryer lid. Grill for 15 minutes per batch and flip the beef every 8 minutes for even grilling.

Meanwhile, pour the marinade on a saucepan and allow to simmer for 10 minutes or until the sauce thickens.

Slice the beef and pour over the sauce.

Nutrition:

Calories 568, Fat 34.7g, Protein 59.1g, Sugar 1g.

Chapter 4: Snacks, Appetizers, And

Desserts

41. Moist Chocolate Cake

Preparation Time: 10 minutes | Cooking Time: 25

minutes | Servings: 8

Ingredients:

1 egg

1 tsp baking soda

1 tsp baking powder

3 tbsp cocoa powder

1 cup of sugar

1 cup all-purpose flour

1 tsp vanilla

1/4 cup butter 1 cup boiling water 1/4 tsp salt

Directions:

Spray a baking dish with cooking spray and set it aside.

Add butter and boiling water in a mixing bowl and beat until butter is melted.

Add vanilla and egg and beat until well combined.

In a medium bowl, mix flour, baking soda, baking powder, cocoa powder, sugar, and salt.

Add egg mixture into the flour mixture and beat until well combined.

Pour batter into prepared baking dish.

Place steam rack in the instant pot then places a baking dish on top of the rack.

Seal pot with air fryer lid and select bake mode then set the temperature to 350°F and timer for 25 minutes.

Serve and enjoy.

Nutrition:

Calories 216, Fat 6.7g, Carbohydrates 38.5g, Sugar 25.2g, Protein 2.7g, Cholesterol 36mg.

42.   Key Lime Pie

Preparation Time: 10 minutes | Cooking Time: 30 minutes | Servings: 1

Ingredients For the filling:

2 eggs

1/4 cup condensed milk

2 tbsp fresh lime juice

For crust:

1 tbsp butter, melted

1/4 cup crushed cracker crumbs

Directions:

Mix crushed cracker crumbs and melted butter.

Add crushed cracker mixture into the ramekin and

press down with the back of the spoon.

Place the dehydrating tray in a multi-level air fryer basket and place basket in the instant pot.

Place ramekin on a dehydrating tray.

Seal pot with air fryer lid and select bake mode then set the temperature to 350°F and timer for 15 minutes.

Once done then remove the ramekin from the pot and set it aside to cool.

For filling: In a small bowl, whisk eggs with condensed milk and lime juice until smooth.

Pour egg mixture into baked crust.

Again, place the ramekin on a dehydrating tray.

Seal pot with air fryer lid and select bake mode then set

the temperature to 350ºF and timer for 15 minutes.

Serve and enjoy.

Nutrition:

Calories 589, Fat 29g, Carbohydrates 67g, Sugar 47.8g,

Protein 18.9g, Cholesterol 384mg.

43. Choco Chip Brownies

Preparation Time: 10 minutes | Cooking Time: 25 minutes | Servings: 8

Ingredients:

2 eggs

1/2 cup olive oil

1 tsp vanilla

1/2 cup chocolate chips

1/4 tsp baking powder 1/3 cup cocoa powder

1/2 cup flour 1 cup of sugar 1/2 tsp salt

Directions:

Spray a baking dish with cooking spray and set it aside.

In a mixing bowl, mix flour, baking powder, cocoa powder, sugar, and salt.

Add eggs, oil, and vanilla and stir until combined.

Add chocolate chips and stir well.

Pour batter into the baking dish.

Place steam rack in the instant pot then places baking dish on top of the rack.

Seal pot with air fryer lid and select bake mode then set the temperature to 350°F and timer for 25 minutes.

Serve and enjoy.

Nutrition:

Calories 312, Fat 17.4g, Carbohydrates 39.4g, Sugar 30.6g, Protein 3.6g, Cholesterol 43mg.

44.   Moist Nutella Brownies

Preparation Time: 10 minutes | Cooking Time: 20 minutes | Servings: 8

Ingredients:

2 eggs

1/2 cup all-purpose flour

1 1/4 cup Nutella chocolate hazelnut spread

1 tsp kosher salt

Directions:

Spray a baking dish with cooking spray and set it aside.

In a mixing bowl, mix eggs, Nutella, flour, and salt until well combined.

Pour batter into the prepared baking dish.

Place steam rack in the instant pot then places baking dish on top of the rack.

Seal pot with air fryer lid and select bake mode then set the temperature to 350°F and timer for 20 minutes.

Serve and enjoy.

Nutrition:

Calories 294, Fat 16.2g, Carbohydrates 32.3g, Sugar 26.4g, Protein 4.7g, Cholesterol 41mg.

45.   Lemon Mousse

Preparation Time: 10 minutes | Cooking Time: 12 minutes | Servings: 2

Ingredients:

2 oz cream cheese, soft

1/2 tsp liquid stevia

2 tbsp fresh lemon juice

1/2 cup heavy cream

Pinch of salt

Directions:

Spray 2 ramekins with cooking spray and set aside.

In a bowl, beat together cream cheese, sweetener,

lemon juice, heavy cream, and salt until smooth.

Pour cream cheese mixture into the prepared ramekins.

Place the dehydrating tray in a multi-level air fryer basket and place basket in the instant pot.

Place ramekins on a dehydrating tray.

Seal pot with air fryer lid and select bake mode then set the temperature to 350°F and timer for 12 minutes.

Serve and enjoy.

Nutrition:

Calories 206, Fat 21.1g, Carbohydrates 1.9g, Sugar 0.4g, Protein 2.9g, Cholesterol 72mg.

46. Healthy Almond Cookies

Preparation Time: 10 minutes | Cooking Time: 30 minutes | Servings: 12

Ingredients:

1/2 cup almonds, chopped

1 1/2 cups almond meal

1 tsp baking powder

1/2 tsp vanilla

1 cup of coconut sugar

1/4 cup coconut oil, melted 1 tbsp ground flaxseed

Directions:

In a small bowl, mix ground flaxseed and 2 tbsp water

and set aside.

In a mixing bowl, whisk oil, vanilla, sugar, and flaxseed mixture until well combined.

Add almond meal, almonds, and baking powder and mix until well combined.

Place the dehydrating tray in a multi-level air fryer basket and place basket in the instant pot.

Line dehydrating tray with parchment paper.

Make cookies from the mixture and place some cookies on the dehydrating tray.

Seal pot with air fryer lid and select air fry mode then set the temperature to 340ºF and timer for 30 minutes.

Bake remaining cookies using the same method.

Serve and enjoy.

Nutrition:

Calories 95, Fat 8.6g, Carbohydrates 3.5g, Sugar 0.3g,

Protein 1.9g, Cholesterol 0mg.

47. Vanilla Brownie

Preparation Time: 10 minutes | Cooking Time: 20 minutes | Servings: 4

Ingredients:

1 egg

1/4 cup cocoa powder

1 tsp vanilla

2 tbsp olive oil

1/3 cup flour 2 tbsp sugar

1/4 cup chocolate chips

Directions:

Spray a baking dish with cooking spray and set it aside.

In a bowl, whisk egg, vanilla, oil, and sugar.

In a mixing bowl, mix flour and cocoa powder.

Add egg mixture into the flour mixture and mix until well combined.

Pour batter into the prepared baking dish.

Place steam rack in the instant pot then places baking dish on top of the rack.

Seal pot with air fryer lid and select bake mode then set the temperature to 320°F and timer for 20 minutes.

Serve and enjoy.

Nutrition:

Calories 207, Fat 12g, Carbohydrates 23.4g, Sugar 11.7g, Protein 4.2g, Cholesterol 43mg.

48. Lava Cakes

Preparation Time: 10 minutes | Cooking Time: 10 minutes | Servings: 4

Ingredients:

2 eggs

3.5 oz dark chocolate, melted

1 1/2 tbsp self-rising flour

3 tbsp sugar

3.5 oz butter, melted

Directions:

Spray four ramekins with cooking spray and set them aside.

In a bowl, beat eggs and sugar until frothy.

Add melted chocolate, flour, and butter and fold well.

Pour batter into the prepared ramekins.

Place the dehydrating tray in a multi-level air fryer basket and place basket in the instant pot.

Place ramekins on a dehydrating tray.

Seal pot with air fryer lid and select air fry mode then set the temperature to 375ºF and timer for 10 minutes.

Serve and enjoy.

Nutrition:

Calories 387, Fat 29.7g, Carbohydrates 26.2g, Sugar 22g, Protein 5.2g, Cholesterol 141mg.

49.   Chocolate Souffle

Preparation Time: 10 minutes | Cooking Time: 15 minutes | Servings: 2

Ingredients:

2 egg whites

2 egg yolks

1/2 tsp vanilla

3 oz chocolate, meled

3 tbsp sugar 2 tbsp flour

1/4 cup butter, melted

Directions:

Spray two ramekins with cooking spray and set them

aside.

In a bowl, beat egg yolks with vanilla and sugar. Stir in flour, melted chocolate, and butter.

In a separate bowl, beat egg whites and until stiff peak forms.

Slowly fold the egg white mixture into the egg yolk mixture.

Pour batter into the prepared ramekins.

Place the dehydrating tray in a multi-level air fryer basket and place basket in the instant pot.

Place ramekins on a dehydrating tray.

Seal pot with air fryer lid and select bake mode then set the temperature to 330°F and timer for 15 minutes.

Serve and enjoy.

Nutrition:

Calories 601, Fat 40.3g, Carbohydrates 50.2g, Sugar 40.4g, Protein 10.6g, Cholesterol 281mg.

50. Squash and Cranberry Sauce

Preparation time: 10 minutes | Cooking Time: 7 minutes | Servings: 4

Ingredients:

¼ cup raisins

2 acorn squash, peeled and roughly chopped

14 ounces cranberry sauce, unsweetened

¼ teaspoon ground cinnamon

A pinch of sea salt and black pepper

Directions:

In your instant pot, mix squash with cranberry sauce, raisins, cinnamon, salt, and pepper. Stir, cover, cook on

High pressure for 7 minutes, divide into bowls and serve.

Enjoy!

Nutrition:

Calories 140, fat 3g, fiber 2g, carbs 3g, protein 4g.

Conclusion

Thank you for reading this cookbook. Inspired by local food culture, environment, geography, religion, and cultural activities, comfort foods have always been treasured by food lovers. Be it summer or winter, these easy-to-prepare recipes are ideal for any occasion.

You're cooking for the family reunion, club meeting, or Sunday supper. You want to make the meal an event, and you want friends and family to feel the love.

Every recipe in this collection fills that bill—and more. Here you have more than 600 mouthwatering, heartwarming, craving-killing recipes, including the favorites named above. We're sure that you'll love them; we've tried them all.

CPSIA information can be obtained
at www.ICGtesting.com
Printed in the USA
BVHW092042250621
610374BV00007B/1146

9 781801 711272